CONDOLEEZZA
★ RICE ★

CONDOLEEZZA RICE

★ REVISED EDITION ★

Mary Dodson Wade

M Millbrook Press • Minneapolis

Millbrook Press
A division of Lerner Publishing Group
241 First Avenue North
Minneapolis, Minnesota 55401 U.S.A.

Website address: www.lernerbooks.com

Library of Congress Cataloging-in-Publication Data
Wade, Mary Dodson.
Condoleezza Rice : being the best / Mary Dodson Wade.
p. cm.—(A gateway biography)
Summary: Introduces Secretary of State, Condoleezza Rice, from her childhood in
Birmingham, Alabama, to her amazing scholarly and musical accomplishments and
involvement in foreign affairs.
Includes bibliographical references and index.
ISBN-13: 978-0-7613-2619-9 (lib. bdg.)
ISBN-10: 0-7613-2619-7 (lib. bdg.)
1. Rice, Condoleezza, 1954—Juvenile literature. 2. National Security Council
(U.S.)—Biography—Juvenile literature. [1. Rice, Condoleezza, 1954- 2. National
Security Council (U.S.)—Biography. 3. Women—Biography. 4. African Americans—
Biography.] I. Title. II. Series.
UA23.15 .W343 2006
355'.03307'092—dc21   2002003412

Manufactured in the United States of America
1 2 3 4 5 6 – BP – 11 10 09 08 07 06

★CONTENTS★

Condoleezza Rice was sworn in as secretary of state on January 28, 2005, after her Senate confirmation hearing, where she was confirmed with a vote of 16-2.

On January 28, 2005, Condoleezza Rice stood before Supreme Court Justice Ruth Bader Ginsburg. While her family looked on, the first black woman in American history took the oath of office as secretary of state.

The secretary of state travels around the world representing the United States. It is one of the highest positions in American government. In this job she speaks for the president. She explains how the United States will act in world situations.

Dr. Rice is one of two women in history to hold the position of secretary of state.

That is far different from the time forty years earlier when Condoleezza Rice first saw the White House. She was nine years old. She stood outside the gate and stared at the beautiful place where American presidents live. "One day I'll be in that house," she said.

That was a very big dream for the little girl who lived in Birmingham, Alabama. In 1963 segregation kept white and black people apart. There were no white students in her school. Only black people lived in her neighborhood. Her family could not even eat at the restaurants in their hometown.

Thirty-seven years went by. Then President George W. Bush asked her to be his national security advisor. She moved into a sunny corner office in the White House. It was just down the hall from the president. Even before she became secretary of state, *Forbes* magazine called her "the most powerful woman in the world."

Growing Up

Those who knew her were not surprised. But still it was remarkable. Her great-great-grandparents had been slaves. Even after slavery ended, African Americans remained very poor. Condoleezza's grandfather, John Wesley Rice Sr., did not own the farm where he raised cotton. But he wanted to go to college.

Stillman College in Tuscaloosa, Alabama, was one of the few places that would accept him. He finally saved enough money to attend. At the end of one year his money ran out. But he did not want to leave. Someone told him that stu-

Condoleezza Rice's friends call her Condi

dents who planned to be Presbyterian ministers did not have to pay. John Rice Sr. told the college that was exactly what he wanted to be. After graduation he went to Birmingham, Alabama, where he founded Westminster Presbyterian Church. Condoleezza says with a smile, "We've been Presbyterian and college-educated ever since."

Condoleezza spent much of her time in children's clubs and youth groups at Westminster Presbyterian Church, where her father was the pastor.

Like his father, John Rice Jr. graduated from Stillman. Like his father, he was a minister, but he worked as a counselor at a Birmingham high school. When his father retired, John Jr. became pastor of the church but kept his job as school counselor.

A talented musician named Angelena Ray played the organ at Westminister Presbyterian. Her father never had an opportunity to go to college, but he made sure that all five of his children did. Angelena taught biology at the high school where John Rice Jr. worked.

They married, and their daughter was born on November 14, 1954. Her mother named her Condoleezza. The name comes from the Italian musical phrase *con dolcezza*. It means "with sweetness."

The Rice family lived in a part of Birmingham called Titusville. It was a middle-class African-American neighborhood. Many residents owned their own homes. Some were teachers like Condoleezza's parents. Others were preachers and shop owners. There was even a doctor.

Activities in the community centered around the church. As Condoleezza grew up, she took part in the children's clubs and the youth fellowship.

Her father worked very hard to help young people. The burly pastor coached after-school sports. He led trips to the art museum. He provided tutors for students who needed extra help with schoolwork. He organized clubs to teach chess and Ping-Pong. He even taught them how to waltz. On weekends there were dances. Growing up in this tightly knit community gave Condoleezza a great sense of security.

She was about four years old when she first saw a white person. It was Christmastime. Her parents took her to see Santa Claus. She sat on his lap, staring at the man in the red suit.

Condoleezza's parents gave their bright little girl every opportunity to develop her talents. She had her

> **Condoleezza Rice has a deep religious faith and attends church almost every Sunday. Among her favorite hymns are "I Need Thee Every Hour" and "His Eye Is on the Sparrow."**

Her father, Rev. John W. Rice Jr. (pictured), and her mother encouraged her to get a good education. She credits her parents for insisting that she work hard to make the most of her talents and abilities.

mother's musical ability. She began piano lessons when she was three years old. She could read music before she could read words. At the age of four she gave her first piano recital.

Her father called her Little Star. He loved to tell about a talent program where an older, five-year-old child had the lead part. Condoleezza thought she should have been given the part. During the performance the star got stage fright. Condoleezza pushed aside the tongue-tied child and sang the song herself.

Mrs. Rice kept close watch on her daughter. She bought all of Condoleezza's Girl Scout cookies. She did not want her child going door-to-door to sell them. Mrs. Rice shopped at the best department stores. The dressing rooms were only for white people, but Mrs. Rice refused to buy anything until the clerk let Condoleezza try on the dresses.

At the age of five, Condoleezza was ready to start school. Her November birthday meant that she would have to wait. Mrs. Rice stayed home that year and taught her. Condoleezza entered public school in the second grade. Later, she skipped seventh grade as well.

Mr. Rice believed that education was a person's best defense. He said, "If it's in your head, no one can take it away from you." Condoleezza's parents enrolled her in many book clubs. Books stacked up beside her bed. The Rices bought new textbooks for Condoleezza's class because textbooks given to schools with minority children were often old and outdated.

Condoleezza's after-school hours were filled with activities. She learned to ice skate. She took ballet lessons. Three times a week she studied French. She continued piano lessons and became so skilled that she was allowed to take lessons at the all-white Birmingham Southern Conservatory of Music.

She did well in everything. Her parents built her self-confidence by including her in family decisions. She got to choose dinner menus and help decide family outings. Their strong support convinced Condoleezza that she could be anything she wanted to be, even president of the United States.

Years later Condoleezza Rice remembered those early years. "You were taught that you were good enough, but you might have to be twice as good, given you're black."

Parents in Titusville tried to protect their children from racism as much as they could. They avoided public buses where they would have to sit in the back. But it was hard to hide the fact that only white children went to the city swimming pools. Minority children could go to Kiddieland amusement park only one day a year. Condoleezza never went there. Instead, she went to famous Coney Island while her father was studying at Columbia University in New York City.

A Time of Change

Condoleezza was about nine when two things happened that made her aware of the struggle for equality. Dr. Martin Luther King Jr. was leading peaceful protest marches in the South. When the marchers came to

Birmingham, the Rices did not join them. Condoleezza's father felt that education was the way to overcome segregation, but he wanted his daughter to understand what was happening.

With Condoleezza up on his shoulders, he stood some distance away. Police arrested many marchers. The state fairgrounds was the only place large enough to hold them. Condoleezza went with her father to check on some of his students who were held there.

Then, on September 15, 1963, a hate group called the Ku Klux Klan set off a bomb in the Sixteenth Street Baptist Church. Condoleezza's church was a few miles away. She heard the blast that Sunday morning. Four young girls were killed. One of them was Denise McNair. Condoleezza had attended birthday parties with Denise.

There were more bombings, but the police did nothing. Her father joined other men to patrol their neighborhood at night. They made sure their families were safe.

Often during the summers, the family traveled to different colleges. John Rice studied to earn higher education degrees. When Condoleezza was eleven, they moved to Tuscaloosa, Alabama. For the next two years, her father served as dean of Stillman College.

At thirteen, she was happy about a move to Denver, Colorado. Her father was vice-chancellor of the University of Denver. Now Condoleezza would be able to ice skate year-round.

Condoleezza grew up in Birmingham, Alabama, where, in 1963, Dr. Martin Luther King Jr. and other civil rights leaders led peaceful protest marches to encourage an end to segregation.

She entered tenth grade at St. Mary's Academy and immediately faced surprises. At the all-girls school, she had to wear a uniform. And, for the first time, she had white classmates.

As usual, she sped easily through school courses. At the start of her senior year, she had enough credits to graduate. She was only fifteen years old. Even so, a counselor at the school did not think that Condoleezza, a black student, should try to go to college.

In the Rice family the question was not whether to attend college, but when. Her parents wanted her to enroll at the University of Denver right away. Condoleezza disagreed. She felt that everyone should finish high school. She solved the problem by doing both. Every day she got up at 4:30 A.M. and raced off to ice skate. Then she went to the university and took two classes. In the afternoon she returned to St. Mary's.

> Even though Condoleezza Rice loves to play classical music, she works out on the treadmill each day to the sounds of Led Zeppelin.

By midterm, high school did not seem nearly so interesting. But she completed her senior year at St. Mary's. Her date for the prom was a college hockey player.

For years, she had spent hours playing classical music by Mozart, Brahms, and Beethoven. No one was surprised when Condoleezza announced that she was going to be a concert pianist. Her proud parents gave her a beautiful Steinway grand piano.

She mentioned that she wanted to attend Juilliard, a famous music school in New York City. Her father cau-

Condoleezza attended the University of Denver, where she graduated cum laude with a bachelor's degree in political science.

tioned her, "You might change your mind." She did not believe that could possibly happen.

She never went to Juilliard because, half-way through college, she did change her mind. She had always been the best at everything she did. She did not want to be anything less than the best concert pianist. "Mozart didn't have to practice. I was going to have to practice and practice and practice and was never going to be extraordinary."

As a music major, she had two other choices. She could teach piano students or she could accompany singers. She did not want to do either. She left the music department.

She had trouble finding a new subject that interested her. Then, one evening, she went to a lecture that set the direction of her life.

Choosing a Path

Professor Josef Korbel was head of the Department of International Relations at the University of Denver. He had been an ambassador in his native Czechoslovakia but fled the country to escape the Nazis during World War II. Eventually he came to the United States. When Communists took over his homeland, he became a fiercely loyal American citizen.

In his lectures Professor Korbel showed how politics affected the way governments responded in times of

Condoleezza Rice's interest in politics was sparked by a 1976 lecture delivered by Josef Korbel (pictured) on the topic of Joseph Stalin and international relations with the Soviet Union.

crisis. Condoleezza heard his lecture on Soviet dictator Joseph Stalin. She knew immediately that she wanted to study the way countries interacted with one another.

She chose to study the Soviet Union. She had always liked Russian music and culture. She read Russian authors. Now she learned the history and politics of the giant Communist country. She learned to speak perfect Russian.

Professor Korbel was impressed with his pupil. She visited his home often. They enjoyed lively political discussions. The professor became a powerful influence in her life, second only to her parents. "I adored him," she said. "He is the reason I am in this field."

Condoleezza was only nineteen years old when she graduated from the University of Denver with honors. She was a member of the honor society Phi Beta Kappa.

The following year she went to Notre Dame University in South Bend, Indiana. She earned a master of arts degree in political science. Then she returned to the University of Denver to study with her favorite teacher. Unfortunately, Josef Korbel did not live to see her complete her Ph.D. degree a few years later.

After receiving her doctorate, the twenty-seven-old graduate was ready for even more intense study. She left Colorado snows for sunny California. She went to study

Josef Korbel's daughter, Madeleine Albright, became secretary of state during President Bill Clinton's term. She moved out of her White House office at the time Condoleezza Rice became national security advisor.

After earning her doctorate in political science from the University of Denver, Condoleezza Rice joined the faculty at Stanford University.

military arms control at Stanford University in Palo Alto.

After she had been there a few months, she gave a lecture. The teachers were so impressed that they asked her to join the political science department. The young black woman took her place among older white men. But no one questioned her knowledge of international affairs.

The classes she taught were very popular. Often she set up mock national crises. Students had to work out ways to respond in order to save the country. These methods earned her a teaching award.

International Politics

During the time Condoleezza was teaching at Stanford, General Brent Scowcroft spoke at the campus. Young Professor Rice asked some hard questions. Scowcroft was impressed. "Here was this slip of a girl. She wasn't cowed by the company she was in. And she made sense."

In 1988, when George H. W. Bush became president, he chose General Scowcroft as his national security advisor. The general immediately telephoned Condoleezza Rice. He invited her to come to Washington to be his advisor on Soviet affairs.

She was in her mid-thirties and again surrounded by gray-haired men. These men in military uniforms listened to information provided by the Soviet expert. The United States president introduced her to Soviet president Mikhail Gorbachev by saying, "This is Con-

Dr. Rice met Mikhail Gorbachev in 1990, the same year he won the Nobel Peace Prize for his work toward world peace.

doleezza Rice. She tells me everything I know about the Soviet Union."

In her new job she traveled with the president when he went overseas. In Russia she set up a series of classes. The *Moscow Times* was very surprised. Condoleezza did not talk about cooking. She talked about missiles.

Tiny, always well dressed, she charmed everyone with her smile and polite manners. Fellow workers, however, discovered that she could be tough as steel. When Russian President Boris Yeltsin came to Washington in 1989, he insisted that he must see the president. Condoleezza blocked the doorway. The world leader was almost twice her size. In perfect Russian she told him that his interview was with General Scowcroft. After five minutes President Yeltsin gave up and met with the general.

While she was serving in Washington, momentous events happened. Poland broke away from communism. The Soviet Union split into separate countries. The ugly concrete wall separating Communist East from free West Berlin was torn down. Condoleezza made many trips to Germany to help reunite the country.

Provost of Stanford

In 1991 she was ready to return to California. She wanted a quiet life. She was tired of dealing with international crises at any hour of the day or night. She returned to Stanford to teach. In 1992 the School of Humanities and Sciences gave her the Dean's Award for Distinguished Teaching.

The following year the thirty-eight-year-old professor was named provost of the university. She now ranked second only to the president of the school. This surprised many people. Every other Stanford provost had been at

Here, in 1991, President George H.W. Bush and Condoleezza Rice speak together in the White House before she left Washington to return to Stanford University.

least sixty years of age. No woman, and certainly no African American, had ever been provost of the university.

Critics complained that she had no experience for this job. Condoleezza saw it as a challenge. "I love this university, and I thought I had a chance to do something good for it."

Some people believed that she got the Stanford job because of her race. She made clear her belief that everyone hired for a job should be qualified to do it. "I've always felt you should not see race and gender in everything. You should give people the benefit of the doubt." Her success soon quieted the critics, but there was trouble at first.

Dr. Rice was the first and youngest woman to be provost of Stanford University.

As provost, she controlled the money that paid teacher salaries and provided student services. She faced a huge problem. The previous Stanford president had spent large sums of money unwisely. The school was $43 million in debt.

She slashed budgets and fired teachers. Professors were angry because they had not been asked to help make decisions. Then she did away with the job held by a popular Hispanic administrator. Mexican-American students staged sit-ins and hunger strikes.

Typically, she did not let the protests bother her. She had studied the problem. She had worked out a solution. She did what she thought best. To her, worrying over things in the past is useless. She summed it up with her favorite phrase, "Get over it. Move on."

While provost of Stanford University, Dr. Rice met Volker Ruehe (second from left), German minister of defense, in 1995.

Her plan worked. Stanford no longer had debts. Even those who had complained admitted that the university was better because of what she did. She proudly displays a paperweight that says Stanford met its budget during the six years she was provost.

She did more than balance budgets, though. Music was still a large part of her life. Her piano was her treasure. Each time she moved, she picked the apartment by first judging where she could put the piano. In Palo Alto she played twice a week with a chamber-music group. Occasionally she gave concerts on campus.

The little girl whose father taught her to love football also turned into a huge sports fan. She had season passes to Stanford ball games. She traveled to other cities to cheer for the team. On one birthday weekend, she attended both men's and women's basketball games and watched a football game. A friend remarked, "She'll watch anything with a score at the end."

As Stanford provost from 1993 to 1999, Condoleezza Rice was a huge fan of the Stanford University football team, coached by Tyrone Willingham, shown here with her in October 2000.

Football is a special passion. She had become a Denver Broncos fan when she lived there. If a Broncos game was not televised, she telephoned a friend in the place where the game was being played. She listened to the play-by-play over the phone. She joked, "I probably would have written more books if I didn't watch NFL Sunday."

Because her parents had provided opportunities for her, she tried to do the same for others. After her mother died in 1985, her father moved to California. Condoleezza and her father started an after-school academy in a poor section of East Palo Alto. The Center for a New Generation serves students in grades two through eight. Every day tutoring and music lessons are offered. Extra help is given to those who want to go to college.

The Center stresses positive attitudes. Condoleezza once talked with a girl who was discouraged about her chances to succeed. The girl knew that 65 percent of her classmates never finished high school. Condoleezza said to her, "What makes you think you have to be one of that 65 percent?"

Her job at Stanford brought many honors. She became a fellow (member) of the American Academy of Arts and Sciences. She served on the board of directors of several companies. She was also on the boards of charities, research organizations, and the National Endowment for the Humanities. But service on these boards ended when she returned to Washington.

Condoleezza had not planned to live on the East Coast when she took a break from Stanford in 1999.

Many people assumed that she would become president of another university. She surprised everyone by returning to Russian studies and to her music. In the summer of 2000 she attended a week-long music camp in Montana. She played classical music twelve hours a day.

Someone asked her if she relaxed by playing music. She responded, "The great thing about playing classical music is that you can't hold anything else in your head.... It's not relaxing to play Mozart or Brahms; it's challenging. But in its challenge, it takes you into another space, and I love that."

Renowned cellist Yo-Yo Ma and Condoleezza Rice perform at the presentation of awards by the National Endowment of Arts and Humanities.

Back in Washington, D.C.

Politics, however, would not go away. While she was in Washington the first time, she developed a warm friendship with President George Bush and his wife, Barbara. Now, ten years later, their son, Texas Governor George W. Bush, was thinking about running for president. The former president invited her to the Bush summer home in Kennebunkport, Maine. That weekend, she met the future second President Bush and his wife, Laura.

The three of them became instant friends. They were near the same age. They laughed at the same things. Condoleezza and George W. Bush were both avid sports fans. In between sailing and playing tennis, they discussed foreign policy decisions that the next president would face.

Their friendship grew. Condoleezza visited Texas many times that year. She went with the Bushes to inspect a ranch in central Texas that they wanted to buy. It was late July. Grasshoppers were everywhere. She could not imagine what they liked about the place. "But once we got in the truck and started going down in the canyons I could see why. Now I really love being out there."

Condoleezza is an avid football fan. She has said that she would like some day to be football commissioner. Friends think she would be good at that. They also suggested that George W. Bush, who used to own the Texas Rangers, would make a good baseball commissioner.

At the Republican National Convention in August 2000, Dr. Rice spoke in favor of candidate George W. Bush for president.

Condoleezza Rice and Paul Wolfowitz confer with Republican presidential candidate George W. Bush at his Crawford, Texas, ranch in September 2000.

One of the things that she liked about George W. Bush was his desire to help children succeed in school. She remembered the high school counselor who did not think she should go to college. "In America, with education and hard work, it really does not matter where you came from; it matters only where you are going."

During George W. Bush's campaign for president in 2000, she helped him form his foreign policy. She coached him during the presidential debates. She warned him to stay on the subject, to make the statements he wanted to emphasize. She compared it to playing classical music or performing an ice skating routine. "You can't wing it," she said.

After George W. Bush became president, he asked Condoleezza Rice to be his national security advisor. He

President George W. Bush appointed Condoleezza Rice to the presidential cabinet position of national security advisor. She worked closely with Colin Powell, whom he appointed secretary of state.

As an expert on Russian international relations, Condoleezza Rice met with Russian President Vladimir Putin in July 2001.

knew that she was brilliant and had experience in foreign affairs. He liked her ability to understand and explain complicated situations. "I trust her judgment," he said.

> **Condoleezza Rice speaks Russian, French, and Spanish.**

As national security advisor, she traveled with the president. One trip took them to Russia to meet President Vladimir Putin. The Russian people loved the fact that she spoke their language. The meeting helped establish friendship between the two leaders whose countries had once been enemies.

Not quite a year had gone by when, on September 11, 2001, terrorists crashed planes into buildings in New York City and Washington, D.C. Many Americans died. Condoleezza was part of the team that worked with the president on how to respond.

Secretary of State Colin Powell, President George W. Bush, National Security Advisor Condoleeza Rice, and Defense Secretary Donald Rumsfeld at the NATO meeting in Prague. This meeting, held in November 2002, welcomed seven formerly Communist nations as members, all pledging to help fight the war on terrorism in the aftermath of the 9/11 attack on the World Trade Center.

The president ordered American planes to strike at terrorist groups hiding in Afghanistan. But he wanted the Afghan people to know that the United States was not at war with them. They had suffered under a harsh government. Hundreds of thousands of packets of food were dropped to starving people in northern Afghanistan. Democracy won. Four years later the country had an elected government. Even women, who had never been allowed to vote, held office.

In 2003, President Bush sent American troops into Iraq to oust dictator Saddam Hussein. Many countries friendly to America did not approve of this action. There was opposition at home as well, but in 2004, George W. Bush was re-elected.

This time he chose Condoleezza Rice to be secretary of state. She had been in office barely a week when she left for a nine-nation tour of Europe and the Middle East. She visited France and Germany, who had not supported the Iraq war. Even though they had opposed the war, everyone was glad that the Iraqis had turned out in large numbers for their first free election.

In Israel, Condoleezza met with the Israeli prime minister and the Palestinian president. She encouraged them to seek ways to find peace and give the Palestinians a homeland. She spoke strong words against Iran about developing nuclear weapons. She urged Syria to withdraw its troops from Lebanon. She encouraged other countries to be involved in solving world prob-

Condoleezza Rice, shown here with President Bush is sworn in as secretary of state in Washington D.C. Rice is one of the president's top advisors.

Condoleezza Rice visits a military base in Kabul.

lems. Everywhere she went she repeated President
Bush's theme of global freedom.

The poised, gracious woman who could have been a
concert pianist charmed everyone with her humor and
style. In Paris, France, she visited with students at a
music conservatory. "You make it sound easy, but I
know it's not. I know you must practice and work very
hard."

One of her first assignments as secretary of state was to tour other countries and meet with top officials to promote positive relations with the United States. In Jerusalem, Secretary of State Rice lays a wreath at Yad Vashem, the holocaust memorial museum.

For Condoleezza Rice, being the best means getting a good education, making the most of your abilities, and working hard to accomplish personal and professional goals.

On her first trip as secretary of state, Condoleezza Rice went to Germany, United Kingdom, Poland, Turkey, Israel, The Palestinian Territories, Italy, France, Belgium, and Luxembourg.

Her trip required the same kind of hard effort. She was up at 5:00 A.M. After working out on an exercise machine, she was off to meet world leaders. Sometimes she visited several countries in one day. She was still going strong when evening came, but the reporters who traveled with her were exhausted. When President Bush made his trip to these same nations two weeks later, she had already smoothed the way.

Some people have called her a role model for girls and minorities. To her, the important thing is to set goals and achieve them. "I'd like to think that I could be a role model for some young white males, too."

Condoleezza Rice has charm and an ambition to succeed. Her father lived long enough to know that she had an office in the White House. Will she one day live there? Many people see her as a candidate for president in 2008. She prefers to concentrate on her present job — "do what you're doing, do it well, and see what comes next."

Still, reporters persist in asking whether she will run for president. She humorously turns the question aside. "I'm going to try to be a good secretary of state, and then, as I've said many, many times, there's always NFL Commissioner."

★CHRONOLOGY★

November 14, 1954	Condoleezza Rice is born in Birmingham, Alabama
1957	Begins piano lessons
September 15, 1963	Bomb kills four young black girls in Birmingham church
1967	Moves to Denver, enters St. Mary's Academy
1970	Takes college courses during her senior year of high school
1972	Meets Josef Korbel, the teacher who most influenced her life
1974	Earns bachelor's degree in political science from University of Denver
1975	Earns master of arts degree in political science from Notre Dame University
1977	Josef Korbel dies

1981	Earns Ph.D. degree in Soviet politics and culture from University of Denver; studies arms control and disarmament at Stanford University; joins faculty at Stanford
1984	Publishes a book about the Soviet Union and the Czech Army; receives Stanford's Walter J. Gores Award for Excellence in Teaching; makes speech that impresses General Brent Snowcroft
1986	Publishes a book about Russian president Mikhail Gorbachev
1988	George H.W. Bush is elected president; Rice is invited to Washington by Brent Snowcroft
1989	Special assistant to President Bush on national security affairs
1990	Becomes senior advisor on Soviet affairs
1991	Returns to Stanford
1993	Appointed as Stanford provost
1995	Publishes a book about Germany becoming one nation again

1998	Invited to Kennebunkport, Maine, to talk with presidential candidate George W. Bush
2000	Advises George W. Bush during presidential campaign
2001	Named national security advisor to President George W. Bush
September 11, 2001	Terrorist attacks on New York City and Washington D.C.
October 15, 2001	Speaks on Arab language TV network, Al Jazeera, to counter statements of American hatred against Muslims
2002	Accompanies Yo-Yo Ma in a concert at the National Humanities Awards
2004	Supported President Bush's policies in Iraq; Campaigned for his reelection
November 2004	Mentioned as Republican candidate for 2008 presidential election
February 2005	On first trip as secretary of state, visited nine European and Middle Eastern nations to restore good relations with the United States

★FURTHER READING★

Bredeson, Carmen. *George W. Bush: The 43rd President.* Berkeley Heights: Enslow, 2002.

Bredeson, Carmen. *Laura Bush: First Lady.* Berkeley Heights: Enslow, 2002.

Blakely, Gloria. *Condoleezza Rice.* Northborough, MA: Chelsea House, 2004.

Cunningham, Kevin. *Condoleezza Rice: U. S. Secretary of State.* Chanhassen, MN: York: Child's World, 2005.

Ditchfield, Christin. *Condoleezza Rice: National Security Advisor.* New York: Franklin Watts, 2003.

Felix, Antonia. *Condi: The Condoleezza Rice Story.* New York: Newmarket Press, 2005.

Reed, Julia. "The President's Prodigy." *Vogue,* October 2001, 396–403ff.

"Rice, Condoleezza," *Current Biography,* April 2001, 74–79.

Russakoff, Dale. "Lessons of Might and Right." *The Washington Post,* September 9, 2001.

Ryan, Bernard. *Condoleezza Rice: National Security Advisor and Musician.* New York: Facts on File, 2003.

Wheeler, Julie. *Condoleezza Rice.* Minneapolis: Abdo Publishers, 2005.

★ INDEX ★

Page numbers in *italics* refer to illustrations.

★PHOTO CREDITS★